Adventures in Sportsland
The Bully Series ™

GUNNER

The Basketball Bully
By Charles Hellman
Illustrated by Robert Tiritilli

The Bully Series
The Football Bully
The Soccer Bully
The Tennis Bully
The Golf Bully
The Baseball Bully
The Volleyball Bully
The Hockey Bully

SportsLand is a magical place high above all the clouds.
Each town has one sport and every game has a crowd.
The net, ball, and basket come alive today
For a game of basketball right here they will play.

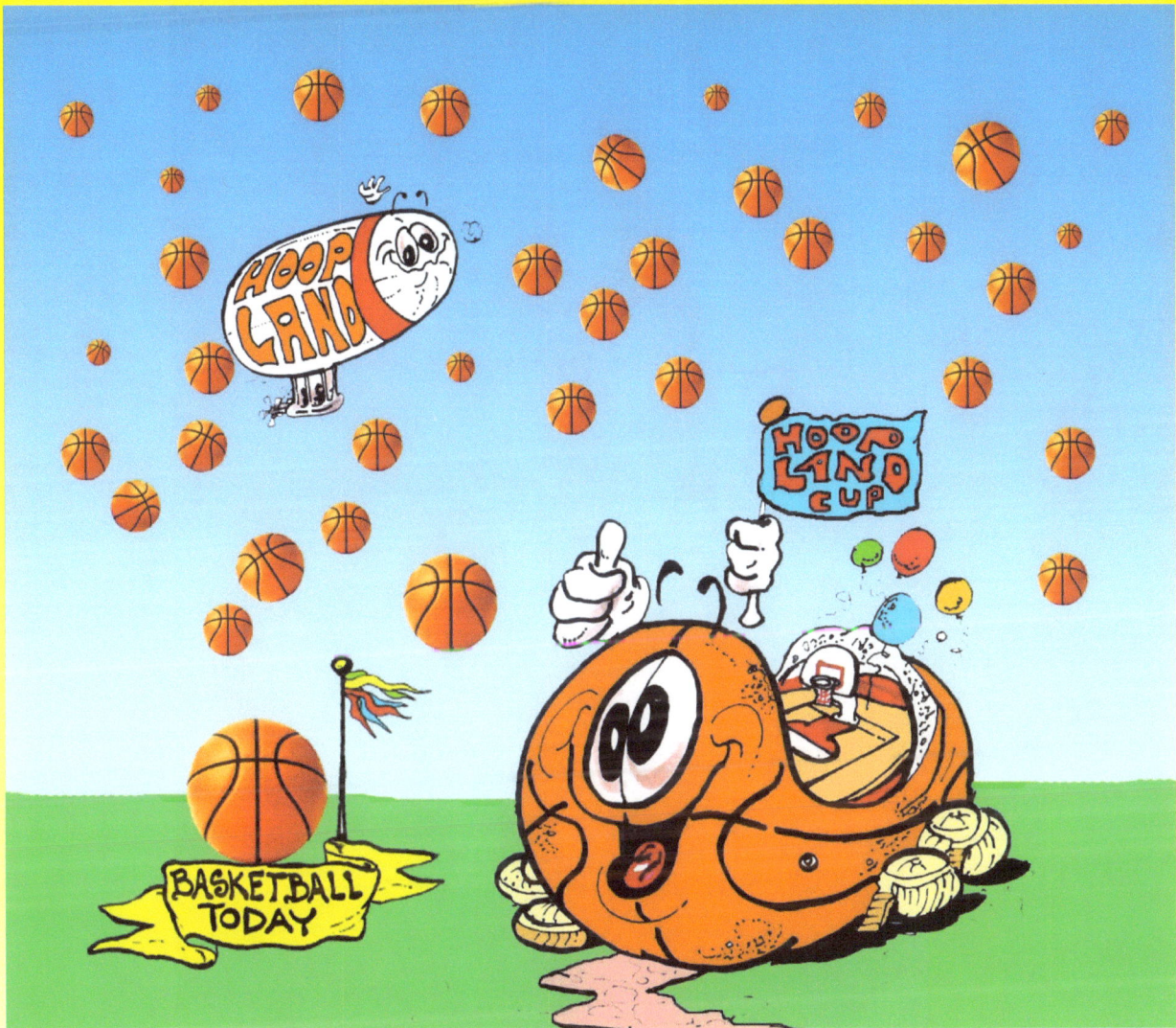

Why all the excitement? What is the reason?
Why - it's the TeamMates' and Hoo-Doos' big game of the season!
The Hoopland Cup game is today
Reads the big blue banner on Bubblegum Way.
Thousands of basketballs - possibly more -
Bouncing in front of the stadium door.

Coach Wiffle and the TeamMates want to play fair.
They follow the rules and always prepare.
Sometimes they lose - sometimes they win.
That makes no difference - they play again and again.
Wiffle tells all the players before they touch the ball,
"Sports are important, but winning is not all."

Wiffle says, "Play well and have a good time.
Learn to pass, shoot, and dribble,
And your game will be fine!
Just have fun and don't worry about mistakes,
But practice those drills and have the patience it takes!"

Coach Trouble and his Hoo-Doos are not very nice.
He cares only for winning and gives bad advice.
Hoo-Doos bully and call names. They trick and they cheat.
They try to act cool. They think they are SOOOO neat!
They use words like - hey losers and hey wimps!
"We Hoo-Doos are better than you bunch of shrimps!"

6

TROUBLE getting MAD!

Loud and obnoxious Trouble enters this place.
When he gets mad, he gets red in the face.
Beware when he winks. Beware when he grins.
That is when he starts tricking and cheating to win.

TeamMates' Locker Room

TeamMates sleep in their lockers and on waking each day,
They put on their shoes and are ready to play!
Hoo-Doos call TeamMates "losers" all through the game.
TeamMates hear their music and ignore Hoo-Doos' shames.

Mike-O'Phone on KFUN radio says to all,
"Bring your teams to the court - it's time to play ball.
The champions will be winners - they will be number one!
They'll get their names on the cup in the Great Hall of Fun!"

9

Mr. TweeT, the referee, talks to them all.
"These are the rules, if you want to play ball.
Remember half court, and the three-second lane.
No double dribble - not in this game.
And this is important - don't talk any trash!"
Then he spins the ends of his long grey moustache.

Hoop de Doo, Dunk, and Gunner are the TeamMates top guns.
They are the favorites of the fans. They make the game fun.
The Hoo-Doos bully all the TeamMates saying,
"You're too tall - you're too skinny
And you are too short for good playing."

At the tip-off, a Hoo-Doo grabs the ball from TweeT.
He gives a big shout and thinks he is so neat.
They never dribble or pass and ignore every rule.
TweeT waves his whistle and says, "You are not very cool."

12

The TeamMates throw in-bound
and Dunk works like a clock,
But there is a Hoo-Doo on a ladder,
and his hook shot is blocked.

Another Hoo-Doo bounces the ball on the floor,
Then goes through the hoop and adds five to their score!

The cheerleaders are Sista, Booma, and Bahama.
Their half-time show adds lots of drama!

Trouble winks and then grins, and you know about him.
Whoa, all of a sudden it is pitch dark in the gym!
Trouble yells at Wiffle, "I'll show you about winning."
Then he sneaks away, and he is still grinning.

In just a few minutes, the lights come back on.
What did Trouble do all the time he was gone?
The TeamMates win the tip-off. They have the ball.
They move down the court. Wow, those Hoo-Doos are tall!

Suddenly the TeamMates are slipping and sliding.
They have no control. All the players are colliding!
There is butter all over! What a sight here today.
The floor is sooooooooo slick that they cannot play.
So much butter Trouble poured all about.
He messed up the floor while the lights were all out.

"Got an idea,"
Gunner says to his team.
"Come and see just
what I mean."

He grabs his lunch box
and gets bread left from his dinner.
"Tie a slice on each shoe,
and the butter will get thinner!"

The TeamMates strap bread slices on their feet.
They lace up their shoes and tie them up neat.
Butter bread shoes - what a fun, funny sight.
The plan works like magic. The floor is soon shining bright.
Buffing the court, they hear Mr. TweeT say,
"The butter is all gone - now the players can play."

The game starts again and Dunk has the ball.
Colored lights bounce off every wall.
Laser beams are everywhere like a carnival night.
Dunk can't see the basket - the flash blinds his sight!
He shoots and he misses with the light in his eyes,
But he gets his own rebound and again he tries.
He scores from his effort - he does not give up.
That is how you must play to win the cup!

21

A Hoo-Doo yells to Gunner, "You're too slow to play.
Watch me - I am going to take that ball away!"
But Gunner dribbles down to the top of the key.
He shoots a jump shot and he scores one more three!

There is a big towel flying across the gym.
Trouble tries to hide, but TweeT knows it is him.
"Watch out!" yells Sista. "You are going to be hit.
That trick towel he threw has hot pepper in it."

Dunk grabs a ball and he is very alert.
He deflects the pepper towel from hitting his shirt.
Instead, it bounces on Trouble and his team.
"Atchoo!" cries a Hoo-Doo, "I can't see a thing.
Not the ball - not the basket - Geez, my eyes sting!"

The Hoo-Doos "Atchoo" while they lie on the floor!
Trouble's trick backfires, as they "Atchoo" a lot more!

The game is tied at seventy-five all.
The Hoo-Doos are frantic to get back the ball.
There is only three seconds to see who has won
And which players will visit the Great Hall of Fun!

While the Hoo-Doos are sneezing, Gunner shoots for a three.
The buzzer sounds as the fans cheer with glee!
Whooooosh goes the ball right straight through the net.
Mike-O'Phone comments, "That's the best shot yet!"

The TeamMates win. What a fantastic run!
They will visit the Great Hall of Fun!
The Hoo-Doos played tricks and they bullied and teased.
The TeamMates played fair, and the players are pleased.
Coach Wiffle says, "Be your best and not rude.
You will always be a winner when not acting crude."

Two Hoo-Doos stop Wiffle after the game,
They talk to the coach and say, "We're ashamed.
We're sorry we teased you and bullied your team.
We don't want to be Hoo-Doos - we don't want to be mean.
Can we be TeamMates if we do not to cheat?
We will play by the rules and obey Mr. TweeT."

Coach Wiffle tells the Hoo-Doos they must change their ways,
"No bullying, no teasing, and no trick plays.
And remember the fair road is the one to choose.
Then no matter the score - you will never lose."

SportsLand is a place high above all the clouds.
Each town has one sport. Each game has a crowd.
The nets, balls, and baskets are now content.
All their time at practice was very well spent.

31

What is SportsLand?

SportsLand is a mystical, magical land where sport is KING. It is located high above the highest cloud, above the highest rainbow and it sparkles brighter than the brightest star. SportsLand sits on a brilliant white fluffy cotton cloud. Look up in the sky, maybe you can see it right now! SportsLand is dedicated to the promotion of all sports for FUN and games are played all day, every day! There are many lands, one for each sport. BubbleGum Way is the main highway connecting all these lands. The road is made of pink bubblegum and it smells wonderful and tastes even better.

What is Adventures in SportsLand?

Adventures in SportsLand's Bully Series is a collection of sports stories that teach children - (who are just beginning to interact with sports teams, coaches, fans and players) - about sports, along with good behavior, confidence building, playing fair and most important… just having fun. These books will help children (adults too!) to better understand how to handle bullies. Bullies in school, sports and playground are timely issues. Bully influence can impact and shape young children's future views of life.

Who are the LuckySports?

LuckySports are SportsLand's inhabitants who cartoon characters in the shape of sporting goods equipment that come alive to play the sport they love. They live in sports lockers where all the equipment is kept. The TeamMates (good guys) and their adversaries, the Hoo-Doos (not so good guys) are the only two teams in SportsLand. The TeamMates obey the rules and the Hoo-Doos try to break every rule.

What is the difference between a TeamMate and a Hoo-Doo?

The TeamMates emphasize good sportsmanship and positive thinking. Their coach, Coach Wiffle, says, "Have fun and learn." The Hoo-Doos and their coach, Trouble, emphasize poor sportsmanship and negative thinking. Envious of the TeamMates, Trouble and Hoo-Doos constantly challenge the TeamMates with tricks, bullying, teasing and other antics. The Hoo-Doos try to discourage the TeamMates in every game, but Coach Wiffle encourages his team to overcome the challenges. The Team-Mates were given life to help others enjoy and participate in sports and improve life through sports.

What is the Great Hall of Fun?

The Great Hall of Fun is a gathering place in SportsLand for LuckySports players that have fun and always try their best. Most LuckySports want to get in to the Hall of Fun, because they laugh, sing, practice, and make friends while there. The Hall of Fun is always filled with loud and happy voices with cool music played from this fun place. Win or lose - the only way to get into the Great Hall of Fun is to show that you have fun and learn how to play the sport.

Characters Matter_{SM}

www.ingramcontent.com/pod-product-compliance
Lightning Source LLC
LaVergne TN
LVHW072121070426
835511LV00002B/55